A CHILDREN'S BOOK
FOR STUPID ADULTS

"TWO THINGS ARE INFINITE; THE UNIVERSE, AND
HUMAN STUPIDITY" -ALBERT EINSTEIN, SUPPOSEDLY

FOR ADULTS 18+
THIS BOOK CONTAINS ADULT SUBJECT MATTER
LOTS OF CURSE WORDS, & SLIGHT SEXUAL CONTENT
THIS BOOK WILL HURT YOUR UNDERDEVELOPED BRAIN

WRITTEN & DESIGNED BY:
Krystal Dawn Jackson
"The Villain Books"

REPORT ABUSE
WARNING
WARNING
WARNING
WARNING
%#!?@

DISCLAIMER

I'M GOING TO PUT A WARNING LABEL SINCE
SOME OF YOU ARE TOO DUMB FOR YOUR OWN GOOD,
BEFORE YOU READ THIS BOOK HEAR ME LOUD AND CLEAR.

DO NOT COME WHINING TO ME WHEN YOU'RE ALL UP IN YOUR FEELINGS.

I DO NOT CARE. I SAID WHAT I SAID. I'M NOT SORRY.
YOU'RE AN ADULT, ACT LIKE IT.

THIS BOOK IS PURPOSELY WRITTEN TO OFFEND YOU.
IF IT DOESN'T, CONGRATULATIONS!
THAT MEANS YOU'RE ALREADY A DECENT HUMAN WITH A FULLY FUNCTIONING
BRAIN CAPABLE OF CRITICAL THINKING, COMMON SENSE, LOGIC, ACCEPTANCE,
UNDERSTANDING, EMPATHY, INCLUSIVENESS, AND HUMOR.

THIS BOOK IS NOT MEANT TO BE A RELIGIOUS OR POLITICAL STATEMENT OR A
HISTORY LESSON. OUR DARK AND SORDID HISTORY IS ALREADY OUT THERE FOR
ANYONE TO LEARN WHEN THEY'RE READY FOR CHANGE.

YOU CAN FIND THIS BOOK HUMOROUS AND THOUGHT-PROVOKING AS IT'S INTENDED
TO BE; SO YOU CAN START TO SEE THE WORLD FROM A DIFFERENT PERSPECTIVE
OTHER THAN YOUR OWN ISOLATED AND SKEWED VIEWS.

OR YOU CAN USE IT AS A TOOL TO SHAME YOUR FLAT-EARTHED BRAIN INTO RE-
EVALUATING ALL YOUR SHITTY LIFE CHOICES.

EITHER WAY, I'M GOLDEN, I'M WRITING IT,
AND YOU CAN SUCK MY IMAGINARY DICK.
YOUR ACTIONS TOWARDS HUMANS ARE WAY WORSE
THAN MY WORDS COULD EVER BE.

REWARD
WANTED
REWARD
100.000$
BEST MOM

WELCOME

WELCOME TO MY "CLASSROOM" BOYS, GIRLS, THEY/THEMS AND ANY OTHER NOT PREVIOUSLY IDENTIFIED LIFEFORM IN ATTENDANCE.

IT'S COME TO MY ATTENTION THAT A LOT OF YOU CAN NOT GRASP THE VERY BASIC CONCEPTS OF HOW HUMANS WORK, OR THEIR RIGHTS TO EXIST.

I'M NOT SAYING ABSOLUTELY EVERYONE SHOULD BE ALLOWED TO "LIVE AND LET LIVE". THOSE THAT BRING HARM TO OTHERS INTENTIONALLY, IE: PEDOPHILES, RAPISTS, MURDERERS, OR PEOPLE WHO DELIBERATELY ABUSE OTHERS, SHOULD BE LEFT IN A CAGED-OFF WILDLIFE RESERVE WITH ONLY EACH OTHER, AND REAL LIFE HUNGRY HUNGRY HIPPOS, TO PLAY WITH.

SADLY, "VIOLENCE IS NOT ALWAYS THE ANSWER" AND WE SHOULD "USE OUR WORDS" *EYE ROLL*

SINCE SOME OF YOU HAVE CLEARLY FORGOTTEN HOW TO ACT RIGHT TOWARDS YOUR FELLOW SKIN SUITS, MAKING ME WANT TO JUMP HEADFIRST INTO A GIANT VAT OF MELTED PEANUT BUTTER MIXED WITH LEGOS, WE'RE GOING TO TAKE A TRIP BACK TO THE PRESCHOOL STORYTIME CARPET AND RE-LEARN ALL THE ABSOLUTE BASICS OF:

HOW TO NOT BE A TOTAL FUCKING DISAPPOINTMENT TO HUMANITY.

I'M EXCITED. ARE YOU?
LET'S GO USE OUR WORDS!

RACISM

HOW CAN YOU LIVE YOUR LIFE WITH ALL WE GO THROUGH IN THIS EXISTENCE, AS A SOUL FLOATING INSIDE A USELESS MEATSACK THAT FALLS APART AT THE SLIGHTEST INCONVENIENCE, VIRUS, OR INJURY. WHOSE ONLY PURPOSE IN LIFE IS TO RUIN THE PLANET, YOUR KIDS FUTURE, AND YOUR EXS CREDIT SCORE. ALL WHILE SOMEHOW CONVINCING YOURSELF THAT YOU'RE BETTER THAN THE NEXT.
LET'S GET REAL HERE...

OUR BRAINS ARE THE MOST USELESS COMPUTERS ON THE PLANET. IT LIES TO AND INSULTS US, GLITCHES WHEN WE NEED IT MOST, LOOPS US IN PAST TRAUMAS, PUTS US IN FIGHT OR FLIGHT TRYING TO HUNT DORITOS AT THE GROCERY STORE, AND SHORT CIRCUITS WHEN WE SEE MOTHER NATURES MARKER HAS COLORED IN SOMEONE ELSE'S MEATSACK DIFFERENTLY THAN OURS.

IF YOU'RE WRONG ABOUT SOMETHING THE BRAINS OWN STUBBORN IDIOCY WON'T LET YOU INTAKE NEW INFORMATION IF IT CONFLICTS WITH THE OLD.
THE BRAIN ACTIVELY FIGHTS TO REMAIN STUPID.
ONLY ONCE WE ACCEPT WE KNOW NOTHING, ARE WE FINALLY OPEN TO LEARNING SOMETHING. HOW FUCKED IS THAT.
IT'S LIKE "IF I THINK I'M CRAZY = I'M NOT CRAZY"
IF YOU THINK YOU'RE SMART...

THEN WE HAVE FUCKING EMOTIONS WHICH CAUSE WARS, ABUSE, AND MISTREATMENT OF ALL KINDS. WE SUFFER IN AGONIZING HELL WHEN WE FEEL TOO STRONGLY,
MAKING EVERYONE ELSE AROUND US SUFFER TOO.
WE OVERINDULGE, OVEREXTEND, AND OVERSTRETCH OUR MEANS TO PLEASE THOSE WE CARE FOR. JUMPING INTO SERIOUS SITUATIONS WITH OTHERS TOO FAST HOPING TO CONNECT OUR FEELINGS... AS IF THEIRS WILL SOMEHOW FULFILL WHAT WE CAN'T EVEN FILL OURSELVES.

WE STUMBLE, MAKE MISTAKES, HURT OTHERS, AND GET HURT OURSELVES. WE LEARN, LISTEN, AND WE GROW IF WE'RE LUCKY.
WE ARE ALL FLESH, HEARTS, VEINS, HORMONES, REGRETS, DREAMS, HISTORY, IMPERFECTIONS, AND HAIR.. SO MUCH FUCKING HAIR.

YOU ARE NO BETTER THAN ANYONE ELSE BECAUSE OF WHERE IN THE WORLD YOU HAPPEN TO HAVE BEEN BORN, WHAT COLOR MOTHER NATURE MADE YOU, OR WHAT ADVANTAGES, PRIVILEGES, TRADITIONS, OR TEACHINGS YOU HAD.

SKIN IS SKIN. HEARTS ARE HEARTS. HUMANS ARE HUMANS.

QUIT BEING A DIPSHIT, GO MAKE A NEW FRIEND FROM A DIFFERENT CULTURE, LEARN NEW TRADITIONS, AND EAT SOME DELICIOUS FOOD, YOU INSUFFERABLE TWAT WAFFLE.

YOU'LL FIND SO MANY BEAUTIFUL HUMANS IN THIS WORLD ONCE YOU SEE THAT ALL OF US ARE JUST SOULS, WITH HEARTS, IN A SAUSAGE TUBE.
WE ARE NOT OUR MEATSACKS.

IMMIGRATION

HATE TOWARDS IMMIGRANTS IS JUST RACISM ON A GLOBAL SCALE, FROM EVERYONE, TOWARDS EVERYONE. FURTHER PROVING HUMANS ARE THE DUMBEST CREATURES ON THE PLANET. HOW IS IT EVEN POSSIBLE FOR EVERYONE TO HATE EACH OTHER WHEN WE ALL WEAR THE SAME USELESS FUCKING MEATSUITS.

"BUT THEY'RE TAKING OUR JOBS!" SHUT THE FUCK UP BRAD. SANJAY AND HIS FAMILY DIDN'T MOVE THEIR ENTIRE LIVES ACROSS THE WORLD, LEAVING THEIR FRIENDS, FAMILY, AND CAREER AS A LAWYER OR PHARMACIST BEHIND, TO DRIVE YOUR DRUNK ASS HOME IN AN UBER, OR SERVE YOUR INNER FAT KID DOOR DASH.

THAT WAS NOT THE FUCKING DREAM, YET THAT'S EXACTLY WHAT THEY DID BECAUSE TO THEM IT WAS WORTH THE MOVE AND HARD WORK TO BUILD THEIR NEW LIFE.

THEN THEY HAVE TO DEAL WITH YOUR PUNK ASS TELLING THEM TO GO BACK TO THEIR COUNTRY ON TOP OF THAT?

THIS WASN'T YOUR FAMILY'S COUNTRY ONCE UPON A TIME EITHER GENIUS, SHOULD YOU "GO BACK" TO YOUR ROOTS TOO? I BET QUITE A FEW NATIVES WOULD LOVE FOR NOTHING MORE THAN ALL OF US FUCKING OFF. YET WE'RE HERE, COMMITTING ATROCITIES AND BEING RACIST SHITS BECAUSE SOMEONE FLED A WAR, WANTED AN EDUCATION, A BETTER JOB, OR BETTER OPPORTUNITIES FOR THEM AND THEIR FAMILIES.

I'D LIKE TO SEE YOU MOVE ACROSS THE WORLD, AND LEARN A WHOLE SECOND LANGUAGE, JUST TO HAVE YOUR EDUCATION WASTED AND GET TREATED LIKE SHIT. YOU WON'T EVEN LEAVE YOUR LITTLE ASS TOWN LET ALONE GO ON A REAL ADVENTURE. I KNOW THIS BECAUSE PEOPLE WHO TRAVEL AND EXPLORE DON'T TREAT HUMANS LIKE SHIT FOR MOVING TO A NEW HOME. THEY WELCOME NEW NEIGHBORS WITH STORIES AND NEW ADVENTURES TO TELL OVER COFFEE.

"BUT THE GOVERNMENT SPENDS ALL OUR MONEY ON THEM!"
DO YOU EVEN COMPREHEND HOW MUCH THE GOVERNMENT TAKES FROM US IN TAXES? HOW LITTLE THEY GIVE TO ANY OF US? ARE YOU SO UTTERLY CLUELESS THAT YOU DON'T REALIZE WHEN SOMEONE COMES HERE TO WORK, THEY ALSO PAY INTO OUR TAXES AND THE ECONOMY? THEY ALSO SHOP AT THE STORES, PAY UTILITIES, AND BECOME HARD-WORKING MEMBERS OF THE SOCIETY YOU CLAIM TO CARE ABOUT.

IF YOU GENUINELY CARED ABOUT OUR SOCIETY YOU WOULD WELCOME DIVERSITY AND OPPORTUNITIES TO LEARN NEW THINGS. YOU WOULD WELCOME IMPROVEMENTS, NEW PERSPECTIVES, AND THE ADDED HANDS TO HELP REPLACE OUR AGING WORKFORCE, TO KEEP OUR COUNTRY RUNNING AS WE'VE BECOME ACCUSTOMED TO. YOU SURE AS HELL WOULDN'T BE MAKING OUR HOME A PLACE FILLED WITH YOUR HATEFUL IGNORANCE.

TRY GIVING A SHIT ABOUT HUMANS FOR ONCE NO MATTER WHERE THEY HAPPEN TO HAVE BEEN BORN, BECAUSE IN THE END, AN IMMIGRANT IS JUST SOMEONE WHO'S MOVED, YOU FUCKING IDIOT.

THIS IS A SAFE SPACE
SOUNDS GAY
I'M IN !
LOVE WINS

HOMOPHOBIA

IT IS BEYOND MY CAPABILITIES TO UNDERSTAND WHY YOU'RE ALL SO OBSESSED WITH WHO'S SMASHING THEIR FUN BITS TOGETHER. I KNOW I ONLY THINK OF THE NAUGHTY SQUASH I WANT TO PLAY WITH. IS THAT YOUR DEAL?

AS LONG AS ALL PARTIES INVOLVED ARE AN APPROPRIATE AGE, AND HAVE ENTHUSIASTICALLY GIVEN THEIR CONSENT TO THE ACTIVITIES ABOUT TO GO DOWN, WHO FUCKING CARES WHO IS FUCKING OR LOVING ON WHO.

BEING GAY IS NOT IN ANY WAY SHAPE OR FORM A MENTAL ILLNESS YOU DUMPSTER BABY, NOR IS IT A CHOICE. I WISH IT WERE A CHOICE THE WAY SOME OF YOU PREDATORY BEASTS BEHAVE, I WOULD NOT HAVE CHOSEN TO BE ATTRACTED TO MEN WILLINGLY.
I AM 100% HETEROSEXUAL AGAINST MY WILL, AND BEST INTERESTS.

THERE IS NOT A DAMN THING WRONG WITH TWO GROWN MEN, OR WOMEN, EMBARKING ON THE JOURNEY OF A LIFE TOGETHER.

ARE YOU JEALOUS THEY'RE GETTING WHAT YOU WANT? ARE YOU AFRAID IF YOU START LIVING YOUR TRUTH, YOU'LL BE TREATED HOW YOU'VE TREATED OTHERS?

"THEY'RE SHOVING THEIR GAY AGENDA DOWN OUR THROATS!!"
YOU WANT WHAT DOWN YOUR THROAT NOW? AGAIN, JUST SAY YOU'RE GAY OR AT LEAST BISEXUAL, AND GO FIND SOME HAPPINESS IN LIFE.

"THEY'RE EXPOSING KIDS TO THEIR SEXUAL WAYS!!"
IS IT "SHOVING SEX IN YOUR KIDS' FACES" WHEN YOUR HUSBAND WALKS IN AT THE END OF THE DAY AND KISSES YOU? WHY ON EARTH WOULD YOU HAVE IT IN YOUR HEAD THAT GAY COUPLES ARE SITTING THERE TALKING ABOUT THEIR SEX LIFE TO THEIR CHILDREN... DO YOU? THAT WOULD EXPLAIN A LOT.

"HOW WILL I EXPLAIN YOUR LIFESTYLE TO MY KIDS? THEIR POOR INNOCENCE!!"
YET YOU CAN TELL YOUR CHILD THAT IF THEY ACT LIKE A HUMAN IN ANY NEGATIVE WAY THEY'LL BURN FOR ALL ETERNITY WHILE BEING TORTURED BY LITTERAL DEMONS BECAUSE THE IMAGINARY MAN THEY CAN'T SEE LOVES THEM, BUT ONLY IF THEY ACT RIGHT. IF THEY DON'T THEN FUCK THEM KIDS, INTO THE FIREY PITS OF HELL THEY GO.

"WELL HUNNY, STEVE AND DAVE LOVE EACH OTHER AS MOMMY AND DADDY DO. SOME MEN LOVE OTHER MEN, SOME WOMEN LOVE OTHER WOMEN, SOME MEN AND WOMEN LOVE BOTH MEN AND WOMEN, AND SOME WOMEN UNFORTUNATELY ONLY LOVE MEN.
AS LONG AS EVERYONE RESPECTS EACH OTHER, ALL LOVE IS A GOOD THING".

SEE HOW EASY THAT WAS YOU LIQUEFIED DUNG PILE. STOP BEING A PERVERT AND TURNING INNOCENT LOVE INTO YOUR ADULT DESIRES.
CHILDREN DO NOT VIEW THE WORLD THROUGH YOUR BEDROOM EYES.
SEX IS DONE IN PRIVATE, LOVE IS LIVED OUT LOUD.
HOPE THAT'S NOT TOO HARD FOR YOUR PEA-SIZED BRAIN TO UNDERSTAND.

TRANS
POWER
HELLO
my name is
NEW
Estrogen
2mg Tablets

TRANSPHOBIA

CLOSE YOUR EYES, AND PICTURE YOURSELF, DOES IT MATCH WHAT YOU SEE IN THE MIRROR? DELUSIONS OF A 6-PACK ASIDE. YOU PROBABLY SEE YOURSELF IN BETTER SHAPE, BETTER DRESSED, BETTER POSTURE. WOULD YOU EVER CONSIDER SURGICALLY CHANGING YOURSELF TO SOMETHING YOU'RE NOT?
WE'RE NOT JUST TALKING SOME TIG OL BITTY'S OR A NOSE JOB HERE.

IMAGINE SEEING YOUR IMAGE IN YOUR HEAD EVERY DAY. YOU TRY YOUR BEST TO BE WHO YOU ARE, BUT WHO'S IN THE MIRROR IS ALL WRONG AND YOU CAN'T DELUSION YOURSELF INTO BEING OK. YOU WANT TO CRAWL OUT OF YOUR SKIN.

OH, YOU'VE NEVER FELT LIKE THAT?
YOU'VE NEVER LOOKED IN THE MIRROR AND SEEN THE WRONG BODY, WRONG GENDER, AND WRONG PARTS LOOKING BACK AT YOU? YOU'VE NEVER WANTED TO SURGICALLY CHOP OFF YOUR DICK, OR GET A NEW SHINY ONE?
BECAUSE YOU'RE NOT TRANSGENDER FUCKWIT.
IT'S AS SIMPLE AS THAT.

"ITS NOT NATURAL! WE CAN'T JUST CHANGE GENDERS"
THE FACT OUR BODIES ACCEPT HORMONE TREATMENTS, AND THEN CHANGE ACCORDINGLY, SAYS YES, YES WE CAN.

EVERYTHING ON THIS PLANET IS COMPLEX, INTERCHANGEABLE, AND EVER-EVOLVING. JUST NOT HUMANS? RIGHT. JUST BECAUSE YOU WANT TO REMAIN IN A PERIOD OF THE 1950S WHEN YOU FEEL "MEN WERE MEN AND WOMEN WERE WOMEN!" DOESN'T MAKE YOU RIGHT. IT MAKES YOU INSANE BECAUSE EVERY GENERATION THOUGHT THEIR LINEAGE WASN'T THE SAME ANGRY DRUNKEN MESS THEY ARE.

YOU DON'T NEED TO BE SO AFRAID OF HUMANS JUST WORKING TOWARDS BECOMING THEIR TRUE SELVES, JUST AS PEOPLE AT THE GYM, OR GETTING BREAST IMPLANTS DON'T SCARE YOU, BECAUSE THAT WOULD BE STUPID RIGHT? RIGHT.

WITH ALL THE HATE YOU GIVE TRANS PEOPLE, HOW MANY DO YOU PERSONALLY KNOW? HOW MANY HAVE YOU PERSONALLY BEEN HARASSED BY? HOW MANY DATES HAVE YOU BEEN ON WHERE YOU WEREN'T FULLY INFORMED OF A PERSONS CURRENT GENDER? HOW MANY TIMES HAVE ANY OF YOUR UNFOUNDED, IGNORANT FEARS COME TRUE?

WHY ARE YOU SO OBSESSED WITH OTHER PEOPLE'S FUCK STICKS? HOW IS THEM LIVING THEIR LIVES ANY OF YOUR CONCERN IN THE FIRST PLACE? IN NO WAY DOES ANOTHER WOMAN'S EXISTENCE THREATEN MINE, NO MATTER WHEN OR HOW SHE BECAME A WOMAN. I'M SECURE IN MY SKIN, AND NO ONES GENDER, CIS OR TRANS, REVOKES MINE.

LET'S NOT FORGET THAT TRANS MEN ARE FINE AF BUT YOU'RE NOT WORRIED ABOUT THEM USING OUR BATHROOMS ARE YOU? ONLY TRANS WOMEN. YOU SHOULD BE.
YOU SEND TRANS MEN TO OUR BATHROOMS...
HE KNOWS WHERE EVERY PART OF A WOMAN'S ANATOMY IS LOCATED, HE WON'T NEED A MAP TO FIND THE RIGHT SPOT LIKE MOST OF YOU MEN.

GET
YOUR
LAWS
OFF MY
BODY

WOMEN

I CAN'T BELIEVE THIS ISSUE HAS BEEN AROUND FOR AS LONG AS IT HAS. Y'ALL JUST A CLUELESS BUNCH OF FUCKING IDIOTS. WOMAN SHOULD BE FEARED, WORSHIPED, AND RESPECTED. INSTEAD, WE SUPPRESS WOMENS ABILITIES OUT IN SOCIETY, AND SEXUALITIES BEHIND CLOSED DOORS. SOCIETY GASLIGHTS, MANIPULATES, CONTROLS, VIOLATES, DISMISSES WOMEN'S ISSUES, AND TREATS US AS PROPERTY TO BE "HANDLED", OR USED, INSTEAD OF THE BEAUTIFUL, LIFE-GIVING, CAPABLE, AND FEARFUL CREATURES WE ARE.

I'D LOVE TO SAY IT'S JUST MEN WHO TREAT WOMEN WITH SUCH DISGUST BUT I CAN NOT BLAME THE STUPID FUCKERS ALONE. EVERYONE'S AT FAULT FOR HOW BADLY WOMEN GET TREATED. WOMEN ATTACK EACH OTHER OVER EVERY LITTLE THING. EVERY SINGLE PERSONAL CHOICE THAT A WOMAN IS OUT THERE MAKING, ANOTHER WOMAN IS HISSING HER TEETH AND JUDGING, USUALLY VERY PUBLICLY UNDER THE GUISE OF "IT'S MY OPINION". YOU LIKING STRAWBERRIES IS AN OPINION KAREN, NOT WHAT ANOTHER WOMAN CHOOSES FOR HER LIFE.

WHY THE FUCK IS IT THAT WE GO THROUGH OUR LIVES WANTING TO BE LOVED, APPRECIATED, AND BE SEEN AS A FULL HUMAN DESPITE OUR GENDER, YET WE CAN'T GIVE THAT VERY SAME RESPECT TO OTHERS. I GREW UP WITH THE BELIEF THAT 'RESPECT GETS RESPECT'. RESPECTING WOMEN GETS YOU RESPECTED IN RETURN, ITS THAT SIMPLE. IF YOU FEEL YOU DESERVE RESPECT OR KINDNESS, HOW CAN YOUR SIMPLE LITTLE MIND FEEL ANY OTHER MEATSACK OUT HERE DESERVES LESS?

IT'S ABOUT TIME WE UPLIFT AND SUPPORT EACH OTHER SO WE CAN STAND TOGETHER, TAKE BACK OUR POWER, AND FIX THIS SHITHOLE OF A FUCKING PLANET.

MEN NEED TO STOP TREATING WOMEN LIKE THEY ONLY EXIST FOR PLEASURE. YOU'RE GOING TO END UP WITHOUT US. THE WORLD IS ALREADY SHIFTING AND YOU KNOW IT, THAT'S WHY YOU'RE SPAWNING THE ANDREW TATES AND PICK ME PEARLS TO TRY AND RE-SUPPRESS US. IF MEN JUST REALIZED WHEN YOU OPEN YOUR MINDS TO SEEING US AS HUMANS, WE NATURALLY COME WITH PLEASURE IN EVERY ASPECT OF OUR BEING. WE RADIATE JOY, INNOCENCE, PLAYFULNESS, BEAUTY, INSIGHTFULNESS, HUMOR, TENDERNESS, AND JUST ENOUGH CRAZY TO KEEP YOU ON YOUR TOES. WE HOLD ALL THE BEAUTY IN THE WORLD UNTIL YOU STOMP OUT OUR FLAMES. THEN WE BECOME YOUR WORST NIGHTMARE, CAPABLE OF MEASURES THAT WOULD MAKE EVEN THE DEVIL RUN IN FEAR.

WOMEN, WE NEED TO DO SO MUCH FUCKING BETTER THAN THIS BULLSHIT, WE CREATE OUR STANDARD OF TREATMENT NOT MEN. NO WOMAN ON THIS PLANET CAN DIMINISH ANOTHER WOMAN'S FLAME BY SIMPLY BEING HERSELF. A WOMAN CHOOSING HER PATH IN LIFE THAT IS NOT A PATH YOU WOULD TAKE, OR ARE PERHAPS AFRAID TO TAKE, CAN'T IN ANY WAY AFFECT THE EXISTENCE OF ANOTHER. WE ARE ALL SO UNIQUELY SPIRITED, AND DESERVE SO MUCH MORE FROM MEN, OURSELVES, AND EACH OTHER, THAN THIS.

LIVE AND LET LIVE, CELEBRATE THE DIFFERENCES, AND SUPPORT THE SIMILARITIES. WOMEN HAVE BEEN TOLD WHAT TO DO SINCE THE BEGINNING OF TIME AND I'M SO FUCKING DONE. DON'T TELL ME SHIT, DON'T CHOOSE SHIT FOR ME, DON'T TRY TO CHANGE SHIT ABOUT ME, SUPPORT WHAT I CHOOSE FOR MYSELF OR YEET YOURSELF OFF A FUCKING VOLCANO LEDGE.

DISABILITIES

FOR ALL THE BEAUTY HUMANITY HOLDS, SOME OF Y'ALL ARE NOT IT. BULLYING THOSE DIFFERENTLY ABLED THAN YOU IS THE LOWEST OF THE LOW A HUMAN CAN GO. HOW IN THE WORLD CAN A FUCKING MEDICAL CONDITION, OR UNFORTUNATE INJURY, MAKE YOU FEEL ANY TYPE OF WAY. I WILL NEVER UNDERSTAND HOW A CONDITION THAT EFFECTS SOMEONE ELSE SOMEHOW GETS YOUR DUMBASS DELICATE LITTLE PANTIES IN A BUNCH.

HOW SAD CAN ONE'S INTERNAL DIALOG BE TO LOOK AT SOMEONE ELSE AND SEE ANYTHING OTHER THAN A SOUL AND CONSCIOUSNESS INSIDE A MEATSUIT THAT THEY ALSO DIDN'T CHOOSE? HOW DOES SOMEONE ELSE'S DIFFICULTIES OR DIFFERENCES MAKE YOU SO UNCOMFORTABLE, OR STRAIGHT-UP ANGRY?

NO ONE ON THIS PLANET, IN ANY SHAPE, FORM, COLOR, SIZE, OR ABILITY, DESERVES TO BE TREATED LIKE LESS THAN. INSIDE EVERY SINGLE HUMAN, VERBAL OR NOT, IS A SOUL THAT DESERVES CONNECTION, UNDERSTANDING, AND KINDNESS. NOT TO BE GAWKED AT AND TREATED LIKE A PUBLIC ATTRACTION.

IMAGINE YOUR LIFE BEING MADE A THOUSAND TIMES HARDER OVER SOMETHING YOU DIDN'T CAUSE, THEN HAVING TO DEAL WITH THE WHISPERS, STARES, SILENT JUDGEMENTS, PITTY, AND INACCURATE ASSUMPTIONS TOO, WHILE NEVER TRULY BEING SEEN FOR WHO YOU ARE.

THE PERSON YOU DEEM AS "NOT ALL THERE" HAS MORE UNDERSTANDING OF THE WORLD AROUND THEM THAN YOU OR I EVER COULD. EVEN WITH SEVERE LIMITATIONS AND DIFFICULTIES THEY SOMEHOW STILL HOLD JOY IN THEIR HEARTS AND SEE GOOD IN A WORLD THAT HAS CONSISTENTLY SHOWN THEM THE WORST.

THE SOUL YOU DEEM AS "UNATTRACTIVE" ON THE OUTSIDE BECAUSE THEY DON'T FIT THE TYPICAL "STANDARDS", LIGHTS UP THE WHOLE ROOM WHEN THEY SMILE, RADIATING GENUINE AUTHENTICITY AND ACCEPTANCE THAT EMBRACES ALL WHO ARE LUCKY ENOUGH TO EXPERIENCE THEIR SHINE. THEY ARE A GENETIC GIFT, A PURE LIGHT IN THE DARKNESS OF HUMANITY THAT WE SHOULD ALL ASPIRE TO BECOME OURSELVES.

THE HUMAN YOU FEEL "LOOKS FINE" AND IS JUST "TRYING TO GET ATTENTION", IS FIGHTING SILENT BATTLES WITH THEIR OWN FAILING BODY EVERY SECOND OF THE DAY, HANDLING INTENSE PAIN WITH EVERY MOVEMENT AND SIMPLE TASK THAT WOULD BRING SUPERMAN TO HIS KNEES, YET THERE THEY ARE DOING MORE THAN THEIR BEST EVERY DAY. WHILE YOU TAKE YOUR BODY FOR GRANTED, THEY WIN WARS YOU NEVER KNEW EXISTED.

STEPHEN HAWKING, HELEN KELLER, FRIDA KAHLO, MICHEAL J FOX, STEVIE WONDER, OR YOUR PRECIOUS HARRY POTTER DANIEL RADCLIFFE, IMAGINE HAVING TOLD THESE PEOPLE THEY CAN'T ACHIEVE WHAT THEY DID BECAUSE THEIR DIFFERENCES MAKE YOU ACT LIKE A FOOL.

YOU HAVE NO RIGHT TO EXCLUDE SOME OF THE MOST UNIQUE, INSIGHTFUL, HUMOROUS, AND INTELLIGENT INDIVIDUALS IN EXISTENCE. YOU HAVE NO RIGHT TO TELL ANYONE HOW THEY SHOW UP IN THIS WORLD, OR HOW THEY NAVIGATE IT BASED ON THEIR ABILITIES. EVERYONE DESERVES TO TAKE UP SPACE, BE SEEN, HEARD, AND RECOGNIZED FOR ALL THEIR GIFTS TO THIS EXISTENCE. EVERYONE HAS A PLACE IN THIS WORLD.

ASKING for HELP is OK
You are not alone

ADDICTION

I HOPE THE MESSAGE IS GETTING INTO THAT THICK FUCKING SKULL OF YOURS THAT WE'RE ALL MEANTSACKS, SKINSUITS, GOO-BAGS, GLITCHEY BACON COMPUTERS, POORLY DESIGNED SAUSAGE CASINGS, OR HAIRY FUN BAGS. WHATEVER YOU WANT TO CALL HUMANS, THOSE SUFFERING FROM A GENETICALLY DESIGNED MENTAL AND PHYSICAL REACTION THAT NO ONE CHOSE, ARE NO DIFFERENT.

IF YOU'VE BEEN FORTUNATE ENOUGH TO NEVER SUFFER FROM HARMFUL ADDICTION, OR BEEN CLOSE TO SOMEONE WHO DID, I DON'T WANT TO HEAR SHIT OUT OF THAT STUPID LITTLE MOUTH OF YOURS. YOU HAVE NO CLUE THE INTERNAL TORTURE ADDICTION CONSISTS OF, A DAILY HELL SOME CAN'T ESCAPE NO MATTER HOW DESPERATELY THEY TRY.

FOR THE FORTUNATE ONES, ADDICTION COMES IN THE FORM OF SOMETHING HEALTHY. WORKING OUT, EATING RIGHT, EDUCATION, CREATIVITY, HOW WE CARE FOR THOSE AROUND US, OR HOW WE CARE FOR OURSELVES. FOR THE UNLUCKY ONES WITH SHITTY GENETICS AND EVEN SHITTER PARENTS, ADDICTION TAKES THE FORM OF SWEET RELIEF FROM THE TRAUMAS OF THEIR REALITY.

WE ALL NEED CONNECTION HOWEVER IT COMES. THE THING ABOUT CONNECTION, OUR INNER BEINGS DON'T CARE WHAT, OR WHO, WE CONNECT TO. SOMETIMES IT'S THINGS OR PEOPLE WHO ARE BAD FOR US. A BAD THAT FEELS GOOD IN THOSE BRIEF MIND-NUMBING MOMENTS.

AN UNHEALTHY ADDICTION CAN NUMB THE PAIN, BUT IT DOES SO MUCH DAMAGE THE OTHER 23½ HOURS A DAY YOU'RE LEFT FEELING NOT ONLY EVERY SCAR YOU ALREADY HAD BUT ALSO THE NEW WOUNDS THAT ARE FORMING. ALL YOU CAN THINK ABOUT EVERY SECOND IS THE ADDICTION, IT CONTROLS EVERY NEURON OF YOUR BRAIN, LEAVING NO ROOM FOR ANYTHING BUT "USE, NUMB, GET SAD, SELF-DESTRUCT, FIND MORE, RINSE AND REPEAT". FOOD, FAMILY, HYGIENE, FRIENDS, APPEARANCE, ALL FADE AWAY. THERE IS ONLY THE NEXT MOMENT YOU CAN LET IT ALL GO, EVEN IF JUST FOR A BRIEF SECOND OR TWO.

IT IS 1000% POSSIBLE TO SUPPORT SOMEONE SUFFERING FROM ADDICTION WITHOUT ENABLING THEM. IT'S NOT ONLY POSSIBLE, IT'S NECESSARY. THE ONLY WAY WE'LL FIX SOCIETY IS BY LIFTING THE MOST VULNERABLE. THOSE SUFFERING FROM ADDICTION ARE OFTEN THE MOST SUSCEPTIBLE TO DANGEROUS PEOPLE OR SITUATIONS, ADDICTION MAKES LISTENING TO YOUR GUT IMPOSSIBLE. THE ADDICTION ALWAYS SCREAMS LOUDER.

THE ONLY WAY TO BREAK ADDICTION IS THROUGH SUPPORT AND HEALTHY CONNECTIONS. IN A DISCONNECTED WORLD FULL OF BROKEN FAMILIES AND FEW FRIENDS, THAT IS NEAR IMPOSSIBLE FOR SOME. FOR THEM THE ADDICTION IS THEIR FRIEND, FAMILY, OR SHOULDER TO CRY ON. THEY LOSE THEMSELVES PIECE BY PIECE INTO A STORM THAT'S SOMEHOW MADE OF NOTHINGNESS, AND EVERYTHING, ALL AT ONCE. THAT IS ADDICTION. IT DOESN'T HAVE TO BE THAT WAY. THROUGH SUPPORT AND COMPASSION, HEALTHY CONNECTIONS ARE MORE THAN POSSIBLE. INNER PEACE IS BUILT DAY BY DAY TOGETHER, NOT FOUND OR FORCED.

DON'T JUDGE WHAT YOU DON'T UNDERSTAND. INSIDE EVERY HUMAN SUFFERING, IS A HUMAN CRYING OUT FOR NORMALCY, CONTENTMENT, COMFORT, BELONGING, SUPPORT, HEALING, CONNECTION, UNDERSTANDING, INNER PEACE, AND LOVE. IF SOCIETY FOCUSED ON HUMANS INSTEAD OF MONEY, WE WOULDN'T HAVE SO MANY OF US TRAPPED INSIDE OUR MINDS.

EVERY SINGLE ISSUE MENTIONED WOULDN'T EXIST IF MEN TOOK CARE OF THEIR FUCKING MENTAL HEALTH AND EMOTIONAL WELL-BEING. THE WAY YOU TREAT OTHERS IS A DIRECT REFLECTION OF YOUR MENTAL STABILITY, EMOTIONAL MATURITY, AND INNER SECURITY. LOOK AT HOW MEN HAVE HISTORICALLY BEHAVED AND THE STATE OF THE WORLD THAT BEHAVIOR CREATED. NONE OF US ARE THRIVING, SHIT'S A MESS, Y'ALL HAVE RUN SOCIETY INTO THE GROUND TRYING TO BE "MANLY MEN". THAT MENTALITY IS DANGEROUS AND CONTINUING DOWN THIS PATH WILL BE OUR DOWNFALL. NO ONE CAN SURVIVE A DEAD PLANET, AND SOCIETY DOESN'T EXIST WITHOUT ITS THRIVING, NOT SURVIVING, POPULATION.

MEN NEED TO FORGET ALL THE TOXIC BULLSHIT PAST GENERATIONS, WHO DIDN'T UNDERSTAND HOW THE BRAIN FUNCTIONS, TAUGHT US. MEN ARE HUMANS LIKE THE REST OF US. EMOTIONAL, HYGIENIC, SENSITIVE, SILLY, SECURE, UNDERSTANDING, JOYFUL, SCARED, MOTIVATED, HARD-WORKING, LOVING, BONE-BREAKING, GOO-FILLED, USELESS MEATSACKS.

AS LONG AS YOU'RE NOT BEING DESTRUCTIVE TO OTHERS YOU CAN BE ANYTHING YOU WANT TO BE AND ENJOY ANYTHING YOU WANT TO ENJOY. YOU ARE ENTITLED TO TAKE UP JUST AS MUCH SPACE IN THIS WORLD AS THE REST OF US. YES, WE MAY PICK ON YOU A LITTLE, YOU'VE MADE SOME PRETTY SHITTY CHOICES OVER THE LAST ROUGHLY 300, 000 YEARS OR SO, CAN YOU BLAME US? WE KNOW YOU ARE MORE THAN CAPABLE OF LEARNING NEW WAYS, WE BELIEVE IN YOU, AND WE ALWAYS HAVE. IF WE DIDN'T WE WOULD HAVE DROPPED YOU OFF AT THE FIRE STATION LONG AGO. START BELIEVING IN YOURSELVES.

THIS WHOLE BULLSHIT "A REAL MAN WOULD" IS SO FUCKING TOXIC AND I'M SICK OF THAT SHIT. A MAN IS WHOEVER HE WANTS TO BE AND IS CONFIDENT IN WHO HE IS AS A HUMAN. HE FOCUSES ON BUILDING HIMSELF, HIS HEART, AND HIS OWN LIFE, WITHOUT WORRY OF WHAT OTHERS AROUND HIM ARE DOING. A MAN IS EVERYTHING, AND ANYTHING, HE WANTS TO BE. THERE IS NO COMPARISON BECAUSE JUST LIKE ALL THE OTHERS, ALL MEN ARE ENOUGH.

IT'S OK TO BE GENTLE AND LET YOUR GUARD DOWN. IT'S OK TO SAY WHEN YOU'RE TIRED, WORN OUT, SAD, NEED A HUG, ARE UNCOMFORTABLE, FEELING LESS APPRECIATED, OR UNMOTIVATED. IT'S OK TO WEAR WHAT YOU WANT, LOVE WHAT YOU LOVE, AND BE EVERYTHING YOU TRULY ARE, JUST ALLOW EVERYONE ELSE TO SAFELY DO THE SAME.

IT TAKES STRENGTH TO RECOGNIZE AND ACCEPT THAT WE'RE AFRAID TO PUT OURSELVES OUT THERE IN THE WORLD WITH NO PRECONCEIVED NOTIONS OF WHO OR WHAT WE SHOULD BE. IT TAKES BRAVERY TO DO IT WITH NO GUARANTEE OF VALIDATION OR ACCEPTANCE. IT TAKES SELF-AWARENESS AND SELF-MASTERY TO LEARN WHO YOU TRULY ARE ONCE ALL THE LABELS OF A FALSE CONSTRUCT ARE STRIPPED AWAY.

QUIT ATTACKING EVERYONE ON THE FUCKING PLANET BECAUSE YOU CANT ARTICULATE YOUR FEELINGS BEYOND "SMASH NOW!". STAN LEE NAILED HULK. IT'S TIME FOR YOU ALL TO BECOME THE EVOLVED HULK/BRUCE COMBO, ONLY USING STRENGTH WHEN NECESSARY, AND INTELLIGENCE AS AN AUTOMATIC GIVEN.
I DON'T EVER WANT TO HEAR OUT ANYONE'S STUPID LITTLE MOUTH AGAIN THAT WOMEN ARE THE EMOTIONAL ONES. ANGER HAS KILLED BILLIONS, AND THE PATRIARCHY WAS BORN FROM GENERATIONS OF BRUISED EGOS AND MANTRUMS. THERAPY ISN'T THAT FUCKING BAD.

REWARD
WANTED
REWARD
100.000$
BEST MOM

IN CONCLUSION

I HOPE EVERYONE TOOK AWAY AT LEAST ONE LESSON FROM THIS.
I HOPE AT LEAST ONE SHITHEAD BECOMES MORE ACCEPTING, HAVING LEARNED SOME GOD DAMN COMPASSION AND EMPATHY FOR YOUR FELLOW MAN. YOU CAN DO THIS, YOUR SKULL JELLY HAS THE ABILITY TO GROW THOSE SYNAPSES. YOU CAN MAKE BETTER DECISIONS, AND CHOOSE BETTER WAYS MOVING FORWARD. GO BE LESS OF A FUCKTARD, AND MORE OF A WORTHY FLESH TUBE.
I BELIEVE IN YOU.

THERE ARE SO MANY DIFFERENT ISSUES I COULD TOUCH ON BUT THE BASICS ARE THE MOST IMPORTANT, AND THE MOST FORGOTTEN. IF WE SHARED A FOUNDATION BUILT ON LETTING EVERYONE LIVE THEIR LIFE WITHOUT HARM, MOST ISSUES IN SOCIETY WOULD DISAPPEAR. EVERY DECISION WOULD BE MADE FROM A PLACE OF WHAT'S BEST, NOT WHAT'S THE MOST PROFITABLE.

AS LONG AS HUMANS ARE SEPARATED, NOTHING WILL GET BETTER FOR ANYONE. EVERY TIME WE DEVALUE SOMEONE ELSE FOR EXISTING IN A WAY WE DON'T, WE SLOWLY TAKE AWAY OUR OWN RIGHTS TO LIVE OUR MOST AUTHENTIC LIFE. TREATING OTHERS AS LESS THAN DOESN'T MAKE THEM SMALLER, IT DEVALUES EVERY LAST ONE OF US, AND OUR PLACE ON THIS PLANET.

OUR BIGGEST PROBLEM IS DISCONNECTION, WE SOMEHOW SEE OTHER HUMANS AS SOMETHING OUTSIDE OF AND SEPARATE FROM OURSELVES. WE ONLY RECOGNIZE WHAT'S INSIDE OUR OWN MINDS AS REALITY, FORGETTING EACH INDIVIDUAL IS ALSO A PRODUCT OF THEIR CONSCIOUSNESS. WE ARE THE SAME, JUST SHAPED DIFFERENTLY BASED OFF OUR EXPERIENCES, PERSPECTIVES, AND LEVELS OF KNOWLEDGE.

THE LIFE YOU WERE BORN INTO, AND WENT THROUGH, DOES NOT MAKE YOU BETTER OR LESS THAN ANY OTHER HUMAN. IT DOES MAKE YOU UNIQUE IN THE SENSE THAT ONLY YOU HAVE HAD YOUR EXACT EXPERIENCES IN THAT EXACT ORDER. MUCH LIKE FINGERPRINTS, WE ALL HAVE A BRAIN UNIQUELY SHAPED TO US, BUT IN THE END, WE ARE ALL FINGERPRINTS.
THE SAME AS THE NEXT, WITH SLIGHTLY DIFFERENT CURVES.

NO MATTER YOUR BELIEFS, THERE IS NO DENYING ALL LIFE IS CONNECTED. YOU CAN FEEL IT IN NATURE, SEE IT IN THE SKY, SENSE IT IN THOSE RARE MOMENTS HUMANITY STANDS TOGETHER. LIFE IS BEAUTIFUL, AND HUMANS ARE NO EXCEPTION.

DON'T BE

I HAVE NO CLUE IF THERE IS A GOD OR MANY. I DON'T KNOW IF WE'RE IN A SIMULATION, OR IF THIS NIGHTMARE TRULY IS OUR REALITY. I DO KNOW THAT IF WE DON'T LEARN TO RESPECT AND VALUE EACH OTHER AS THE HUMAN RACE, WE WILL NEVER IMPROVE THIS WORLD, COMING TOGETHER TO SHAPE IT TO WHAT WE, AND THE EARTH, ACTUALLY NEED.

WE DO NOT GET TO DECIDE WHAT OTHER PEOPLE CHOOSE TO DO WITH THEIR LIVES, WHO THEY BECOME, OR WHO THEY LOVE. EACH HUMAN HAS THEIR SHINE AND PURPOSE. MANY OF US GET DULLED OVER TIME. WE GET WORN DOWN BY OTHERS WHO ABUSE, BULLY, OR WANT US TO CONFORM SO WE THINK LIKE EVERYONE ELSE. WE LOSE WHAT MAKES US SPARKLE. DON'T BE THE REASON SOMEONES LIGHT GOES OUT.

IN SOME WAYS HUMANITY HAS COME SO FAR, IN OTHER AREAS, WE'RE STILL IN THE STONE AGES, SCARED OF EVERY SHADOW OR CREATURE THAT LOOKS UNFAMILIAR. YES, SOME OF THIS WORLD, AND THE PEOPLE IN IT ARE SCARY, I KNOW THIS VERY VERY WELL. DESPITE HAVING FIRST-HAND EXPERIENCE WITH THE MONSTERS I STILL BELIEVE MOST OF THIS WORLD, AND MOST OF THE HUMANS INHABITING IT, ARE FULL OF WARMTH AND JOY.

I'M NOT SAYING BLINDLY TRUST EVERYONE WHO COMES YOUR WAY, THAT'S IMPOSSIBLE GIVEN THE STATE OF THE WORLD AND THE BROKEN HUMANS WITHIN IT. YOU DON'T HAVE TO ALLOW SOMEONE THE SPACE TO HURT YOU, TO SHOW KINDNESS. IF YOU CAN'T AT LEAST DO THAT, THEN REMEMBER THE OLD SAYING "IF YOU HAVE NOTHING NICE TO SAY, THEN SHUT THE FUCK UP"

IN A WORLD OF HEALING INDIVIDUALS, YOU DON'T NEED TO MAKE SOMEONE ELSE'S HEALING HARDER JUST BECAUSE YOU'RE STILL AN ANGRY TROLL WHO JUMPS AT UNFAMILIAR SHAPES AND COLORS. LIVE AND LET LIVE. MORE IMPORTANTLY, HEAL YOURSELF AND ALLOW HEALING FOR OTHERS.

MAYBE IF WE CAN GET THAT ONE THING RIGHT, WE'LL FINALLY HAVE A WORLD IN WHICH WE'RE ALL HAPPY AND SAFE. MAYBE OUR KIDS WILL BE ABLE TO EXIST IN PUBLIC SPACES, OUR WOMEN WILL BE ABLE TO TRUST MEN, OUR MEN WILL BE ABLE TO ALLOW THEMSELVES TO BE VULNERABLE, AND EVERYONE IN BETWEEN WILL HAVE THE RIGHT TO A PEACEFUL EXISTENCE ON THIS FLOATING ROCK THAT COULD VANISH AT ANY MOMENT; OR LAST FOREVER, BOTH A TERRIFYING THOUGHT IF WE DON'T GET HUMANITY TO ACT RIGHT.

A FUCKING CUNT

AS I SAID THIS ISN'T MEANT TO BE POLITICAL OR RELIGIOUS. EVERYONE IS ALLOWED TO GO WHERE THEIR SOUL IS DRAWN TO, JUST DON'T BE A FUCKING CUNT TO EVERYONE ELSE BECAUSE OF YOUR BELIEFS. WE COVERED THIS. TAKE THE SAME MESSAGE, AND APPLY IT TO HOW YOU CHOOSE TO LIVE YOUR LIFE REGARDING WHO CREATED IT.

THE SAME FOR POLITICS. NO MATTER WHAT PARTY IS IN OFFICE, THEY'RE GOING TO FUCK UP AND WE'RE GOING TO ARGUE THAT THE OPPOSITION WOULD HAVE DONE BETTER... THEY NEVER DO.
OUR EXPERIENCES AND EXPOSURE TO THE WORLD WILL DETERMINE WHAT POLITICAL PARTY WE SIDE WITH, AND THAT DECISION IN NO WAY SHOULD HAVE YOU OUT HERE ACTING A FUCKING FOOL FOR YOUR "LEADER" BECAUSE OF DIFFERENT SOCIAL VALUES.

IN CASE NO ONE TOLD YOU, IT'S COMPLETELY POSSIBLE TO ENGAGE IN CIVIL CONVERSATIONS DEBATING YOUR DIFFERENCES IN A HEALTHY WAY. UNFORTUNATELY, I DON'T SEE THE MAJORITY OF YOU DOING THAT... *COUGH COUGH* *TRUMP SUPPORTERS* *COUGH COUGH*

OUR DIFFERENCES, JUST LIKE OUR SIMILARITIES, MAKE THIS WORLD THE BEAUTIFUL, MAGICAL PLACE IT IS. COULD YOU IMAGINE THE ENTIRE WORLD LOOKING LIKE A PERFECTLY CURATED VERSION OF THE SUBURBS... THEY'VE MADE MOVIES ABOUT THAT... ITS TERRIFYING.

WE ALL HAVE SOMETHING ABOUT US THAT ADDS SUBSTANCE TO THIS WORLD. WE'RE ALL BORN WITH ENDLESS POSSIBILITIES TO ENRICH SOCIETY FOR GENERATIONS TO COME, BUT NOT IF WE NEVER GET THE OPPORTUNITY TO UNDERSTAND OUR FULL CAPACITY.
STOMPING OUT JUST ONE PERSON'S FLAME COULD BE THE WORST THING TO HAPPEN TO ALL OF US. YOU NEVER KNOW WHO THEY COULD HAVE BECOME HAD THEY JUST KNOWN LOVE, ENCOURAGEMENT, AND SUPPORT.

NO ONE SHOULD EVER FEEL ALONE.
NO ONE SHOULD EVER FEEL LESS THAN.
NO ONE SHOULD EVER THINK THEY'RE NOT ENOUGH.
NO ONE SHOULD EVER WONDER WHY THEY'RE NOT LOVED.
WE ARE ALL IN THIS TOGETHER.
THIS IS ALL OUR HOME.
TIME TO ACT LIKE IT.

THE
END